Nobuko

伸
子

A Memoir

Nobuko (Kathy) Plantamura

Soul Attitude Press

Soul Attitude Press

Pinellas Park, FL

www.soulattitudepress.com

ISBN 978-1-946338-04-4

Printed in the United States of America

To my Ancestors,
my Children, Gregory and Dean,
my Grandchildren, Maya and Foster,
and my Husband, Bill.

Introduction

Where were you born? How long have you lived here?

I have been asked those questions many times and have become accustomed to them. When I convey my history to people, they say, "You should write a book."

Writing had been an interest of mine since I was in my teens but I did not know how to write a memoir. One day at the library I bumped into a lady who wore a tee-shirt that said "Memoir Writing". That lady, Jan Golden, introduced me into a Story Circle Creative Writing Class where she taught. Later when I came to publish my story, John Rehg, the publisher could not have been more kind and patient in assisting me.

When I compiled my written pieces, I decided to call this book NOBUKO. Although most of my friends would call me Kathy, Nobuko was my given name at my birth so the sound of that name is dear to me. I want following generations in my family to read my story and to know how I lived in my time.

Now that I am in my retirement it is quite an appropriate time to reflect on my life and appreciate all the beauty of this universe.

I hope my family will enjoy my legacy and be inspired to write their own with passion. To all my friends who encouraged me to make this book, I am extending my thanks.

Then my appreciation to my son, Gregory, for his assisting me all the way through with the manuscript. Finally, my love to my husband, Bill, for sharing his enthusiasm and great support as always.

I am grateful to all.

Table of Contents

Bill

"Oh, look, look, there they are!" The tourists in Times Square pointed to the huge smoke rings coming from the mouth of a man on the Camel Cigarette billboard.

"Hi, Lee!" I stepped into an Asian gift shop below that billboard. Lee was the shop clerk with whom I became acquainted through a former classmate.

"Oh, what are you doing here today?" Lee looked up with surprise. She was a happily married and charming person from Korea.

"Well, this is my day off and I had no particular place to go, so I took a train and came into the city."

"Say, there is someone I want to introduce to you," said Lee smiling.

"Who?" I asked, intrigued.

"A fella recently came home from Korea, the military service, you know. He is from the

Bronx and come from an Italian family. He stops here sometimes just to browse around."

"Oh, what is he interested in?" I was more inquisitive.

"You know, he is still passionate about Asian culture," she shrugged.

Customers walked in, so Lee went to attend to them. The customers left, then Lee came back and said, "I think he is about 25 years old. He usually stops by on Thursdays, so come next Thursday, won't you?"

"Um … I have an appointment next week, but I can make it the following Thursday. I can probably be here about 2:00 p.m."

I distinctively marked with red ink on my calendar the first week of May 1961 Thursday to visit Lee's store.

The train ride into the city on that day was a little different from the usual – I was optimistic.

"Hey, Lee, I am here. How are you?" I called cheerfully.

"Hey, I am glad you are here!" Lee raised her hands enthusiastically.

"Did you see that fella since?" I asked eagerly.

"Yeah, he said he is looking forward to meet you, so he will be here soon." A young guy walked in. He wore black-framed glasses and a blue plaid shirt neatly tucked into his jeans. He looked straight at me and said, "Are you Kathy? I am Bill." He seemed clean cut and casual. His friendly expression caught my liking and we shook hands. Lee was busy serving customers but acknowledged us and winked. "Would you like to go for a cup of coffee?" Bill asked. "That will be good," I said and we stepped out from the store.

Bill told me that he was in the service for two years in Korea and was discharged a few weeks ago. I told him I am Japanese. Korea and Japan are so geographically close and share similar cultures that they are often confused, although they are separate countries. To my surprise, he was very aware of what I said. Then he spoke candidly about his experience of learning its history, and the 38th parallel – DMZ dividing line. Unexpectedly, I gained some knowledge. When people can talk and educate me, I am always impressed. He looked delighted. I assumed that he appreciated that someone listened to what he wanted to talk about.

Bill said, "Can we meet again next Thursday?" So the following week, we met again. Columbia University campus was one of the places I always wanted to get a glimpse of, because I had heard many Japanese scholars attended there on study abroad programs. Bill was carrying a couple of textbooks under his arm as he took me there by subway. Since it is an American private Ivy League school, I sensed elitism in the air. Bill however was on his way to the local City College. I wondered how different the careers might be for the Ivy League graduates vs. local college graduates.

It was time for Bill to catch a train for his classes. He and I went down the subway steps. "See you next week, okay?" We both nodded and went our separate ways.

It was a privilege for me to be taken places in Manhattan by a native and I felt a sense of immense assurance being with him. I liked the way we were meeting, rather than going to fancy restaurants or Broadway shows, but getting valuable knowledge, that was what I liked best. Each time we met my feeling of confidence in him and comfort of leaning on him increased.

By 5:00 p.m. I was on the train returning to my sponsor family in Long Island. However, I had something to look forward to from this week to the next. While the train was moving I had some thoughts about the person whom I met that afternoon and modestly fantasized about the upcoming Thursday. "He is someone good to have as a friend and I want to be a friend with him," I murmured and closed my eyes. The sun was going down and my day off was coming to an end. Meanwhile I was wondering where this interracial friendship would take us in the early 1960s. In the back of my mind I wondered if my future with Bill was like the illusion of the billboard. Could it disappear like those mysterious rings? Not having any clue to this acquaintance was the beauty of the mystery.

Regrets

"Excuse me?" My voice was loud and argumentative. "Really!" I was startled by the rejection.

The passport, the visa, and affidavit of financial support; they were all spread out on his desk. The immigration officer raised his head. He looked into my face through those Benjamin Franklin bifocals.

"Umm, your request is unacceptable." He shook his head.

The officer read my expression and most likely he felt sympathetic. When your visa gives you the privilege of being in the country, the immigration office can be powerful. However, he said to me, "You have two weeks to alter the status or be deported." He gathered my documents and handed them back to me. I stood there speechless, blood rushing up to my head.

It was 1960 and I had returned to the U.S.A. from Japan, thanks to the effort of Mr. & Mrs.

Hoffman. The Hoffmans were American and also more importantly, I was like their extended family and they were a second family to me. October of 1959, when I left them to go home to Japan, I was assured by the Hoffmans, "Kathy, remember! You can come back anytime because we count you as a family. Sorry to see you go."

Prior to obtaining that visa, when I wrote, "I already miss American life and wish to return to your family," I had told Mr. & Mrs. Hoffman about my motive. That was, I wanted more education. I truly believed that attending the classes was the way to promote my life. Therefore, it was my quest, perhaps on my free time or some evenings, to pick up some kind of courses.

They took me back without any questions. In those days, foreigners could apply for a temporary business visa to expedite obtaining a visa if you were in a business connection. Mr. Hoffman's office did just that for me and my visa was promptly granted.

In gratitude for getting me back into the U.S.A. and having me live with them, I often contributed to their housework. I did the same in my previous stay under the student visa while attending high school. Helping out in any case was my pleasure and the least I could do to show my appreciation.

So I had been away from them almost a year. Meanwhile the Hoffmans had built an estate on the hill overlooking Long Island Sound and the neighborhood was more secluded. There was a young European house-keeper who welcomed me with a smile. Their home showed their abundant prosperity and of course I complimented them. What had not changed was my loyalty and appreciation for them. But I did miss the intimacy of the community where they lived previously where I attended the high school.

My plan for attending two or three nights a week at a local school did not transpire. Each time I inquired about my pursuit, it seemed ignored. Was it because I would have to commute to classes at night and I did not have a driver's license nor owned a car? Whatever, there was a weary atmosphere. I needed to see the light at the end of the tunnel. "One of these days, I want to be independent," I thought to myself every night as I got into my bed.

Since I was not asked, I did not report to the Hoffmans what the immigration officer had said about my visa renewal.

Then it dawned on me – the immigration officer's order, "Two weeks to alter the status or be deported."

"Look, hurry! You can still do something to alter the status! You have a few more days left," I convinced myself. This return to the U.S.A. was focused upon establishing my future. Therefore, under no circumstances would I choose to be deported. I went to Manhattan for job hunting on my day off. I walked in from one building to the next, checking every Japanese business and flipping through the yellow pages at the nearby drugstores to call them.

I couldn't believe it when a director of the personnel department responded to my call. At last my effort paid off. My attitude was persuasive, "I happened to be in town and appreciate it if you can give me an interview this afternoon." My heart was beating fast as I spoke. My inner voice cheered and encouraged me. "Go girl, you have that blue dress on today! You look good. You can do it!"

Great interview! I was hired on the spot. "A giant company is going to sponsor me now," it was surreal. Technically I was transferring the sponsorship away from the Hoffmans to Japan's well-known company, Marubeni, on my own.

The feeling of uncertainty started to creep up on me like spiders crawling from my legs. I shook my head to deny what I was about to put myself through.

With heartbreaking determination I rode home to the Hoffman's, anticipating what I was going to face once I got there.

"How dare you!" the earsplitting voice of my sponsor almost shook the house. "Going to get a job somewhere else behind our back! You'll see! You'll see!" The shouting of the threats and extortions went on. Nonetheless my mind was blank. This ordeal was expected, therefore, I was ready.

The next morning, my guilty conscience was beating me up. "You are the one who pleaded to be invited back and they supported you. If you opt to leave them, that will be a stab in their back. You lose the trust of many good people who supported you to come to this country in the first place." Yes, I felt guilty like an actual criminal. I might as well be a defector who should be kicked off from the edge of a high cliff with the burden of shame.

Yet, I had to do what I had to do to stay in this country, to alter the status on my visa and to seek for my own future which was thoroughly my own responsibility.

Bill was my true friend in my hour of need that night. He came to drive me away from that house while they were out for a dinner event. I said goodbye to the housekeeper, who understood my goal, so she wished me good luck. It was done. In spite of that, I still have a deep scar of regret in my heart. However, this led me to go on an independent life and to find my own American Dream.

1945

"What are you looking for?" I asked Grandma. She had spread out the bank books, government registrations, family photos, and other important looking papers. "Certain documents are going to be necessary when we go home to Japan," Grandma looked very intense. "Why do we have to go to Japan?" I asked; I was six years old.

Although I was born in Korea, our origin was as proud imperial Japanese citizens and nothing more. Grandma tried to explain to me that we lost the war and all our colonial properties. We had no right to live there anymore. Korea was now liberated from Japanese power. "So when are we leaving?" I asked. "Oh, as soon as possible but we shall wait until the baby is born," Grandma explained. My mother was five months pregnant and it was only three months ago that my father had passed away from jaundice.

Meanwhile, needless to say, Korean citizens were celebrating their independence. We were in fear of the resentful civilians as they came to bang on our doors during the night. I felt as if we were getting harassed by demons.

The awaited baby came in November. The sun was going down and the wind felt cold to my face. The whole atmosphere was calm and lonely. We carried what we could and departed from the port of Busan, South Korea. The ship sailed over the Tsushima Strait quietly under the full moon. The soft waves were reflecting the shiny silvery moon. The urn of my father was packed with care in one of our bundles so he too was going home to the country where he started from.

At last the ship docked and we were home, our mother country. The town's volunteers came to meet us and took us to their homes for the night. I will never, ever forget that kindness as long as I live. I do believe in giving and getting back. So even though the situation of the country was in such chaos, there were good people who cared for others.

From then on we were called "Repatriates, the people returned to their country of origin." We found our way to Kure City, Hiroshima where Grandma lived prior to her life in Korea. We managed to trace down Grandma's nephew but we felt unwelcomed. Even though we thought we had returned home, we found ourselves homeless. We had to face the harsh reality. They spared us one night's stay, then the next morning we were off to find our own way. It was not a time to lean on anybody's shoulder. One had to be resilient and become self-sufficient. I never regret those days of hardship because it only helped me to grow up strong and to manage through life. After the harsh winter, always comes the delightful spring. That is the rule of nature. Courage and determination brought us this far and I am appreciative for every stage of my past.

Family photo

Nobuko is pictured with her family in 1949 after their return to Japan. They are, from left, her mother Teruko; Nobuko; grandmother Hanaye and brother Michikuni.

A Letter Changed My Life Direction

The letter came from my Uncle Takeo whom I met for the first time in Tokyo only a couple of months previously. I was 15 then. He worked at B. Inter-national Corporation. He wrote to our family:

> *Please think about it. This might be a great opportunity for Nobuko. If you do not agree to this matter, I understand, and we can drop the subject.*

Although I am called Kathy in the United States, my given name at birth was Nobuko.

> *Mr. Naka, CEO of my company asked me if I knew of a good candidate who is willing to go to New York to assist a family with a newborn baby. I was startled for a moment by such a question. Then I had a quick answer. Nobuko came into my mind.*

As I understood it, the story went like this: Mr. Naka had a lunch with Mr. Hoffman, who lived in New York. They talked casually. Mr. Hoffman said he and his wife were expecting their first child in a few months. "Now on we are going to need a babysitter. Do you have a good babysitter when you guys go out?" Mr. Hoffman awaited Mr. Naka's answer.

Mr. Naka was at ease and said, "We have a built-in babysitter/maid."

"What do you mean, built-in?"

"In Japan, there are many young girls who put their hope into making a career in Tokyo. As a stepping stone, they work as a live-in maid. In some cases, they stay until they get married. Most likely the master will reward her loyalty by finding an appropriate spouse. And furthermore he will see to her wedding, and treat them as an extended family."

"That doesn't seem to fit into our culture," said Mr. Hoffman.

Mr. Naka was a senior over Mr. Hoffman by about 10 years, so he usually had a good outlook and good advice.

"You are kidding! A Japanese babysitter back in New York?" Mr. Hoffman laughed.

But, after a moment of silence, Mr. Naka changed his expression and said, "It could happen! Find a high school girl in Japan and have her come to your home."

"No, that's impossible," Mr. Hoffman thought that it was ridiculous.

Mr. Naka raised his index finger as he seriously said, "Do you know how many Japanese youths wish to go to America?"

Mr. Hoffman looked at the finger of Mr. Naka. "How do you handle that sort of arrangement with the immigration department?"

The answer of Mr. Naka was swift. "As a student!"

"You mean we will get a girl to go to school?"

"Sending her to high school, your benefit is outside of her school hours, she will be your babysitter."

"I see. So we could get a built-in baby-sitter!" Mr. Hoffman raised his eyebrows.

"You will see. Japanese girls are loyal to you," Mr. Naka assured him.

"Well, I will call my wife tonight and tell her this bizarre story but she'll say, 'Are you going nuts?'"

Their lunch was over. Mr. Naka patted Mr. Hoffman's shoulder, "If you want, I will try to help you to find a good candidate." Mr. Hoffman had to get ready to fly back to New

York the next morning.

The letter was surreal to us. Uncle Takeo wanted to see how we felt about this inquiry.

"No, it's a trap!" my mother said and she would have nothing to do with that letter.

Uncle Takeo was my father's younger brother. He was called into the war in early 1940. I remember the days my father and I sent care packages to him in Burma. After the war, he came home to Tokyo and found a job at B. International Corporation. His mind was exposed to the world and I liked that sort of modern personality.

My father had passed away when I was about five. So after WWII, we lived in Kure City, near Hiroshima, Japan where my mother's side of family was from. The four of us, my grandmother, mother, a brother and myself, tried to make ends meet each day. There was no money for me to get a higher education. Uncle Takeo was worried about us in this postwar disadvantaged situation. He wanted to take an opportunity with this letter to help.

I was a mature and adventurous teenager, ready to take on any hardships from life. All the people surrounding me were skeptical with worries and said, "At 15, you are too young to go to America. You don't know their culture and language. We are not sure if you can come home, and moreover, this is unethical." Uncle Takeo did not get a smile from anyone, even from his own wife.

However, my trust in Uncle Takeo's heartfelt offer was deep. I believed in myself to conquer this challenge. This was my life and my own responsibility and nobody else's.

My grandmother always had faith in me and we were bonded for life. Uncle Takeo, my grandmother and myself, The Three Musketeers, as I would like to call ourselves, had to battle out this state of affairs. We left the speculations and postulations to proceed for what we had to do.

Uncle Takeo would talk to his C.E.O., Mr. Naka, then, during the international business phone call, Mr. Naka would slip in my agenda to his counterpart Mr. Hoffman in New York. Finally the updates would come from Uncle Takeo to me. It seemed like a long-winded procedure to me as I was counting the days in anticipation.

Nonetheless, my quest to cross the Pacific to the Atlantic Ocean was granted. The freight ship left the dock early May, 1955. The morning sky was dull but there was sunshine in my heart as I stood at the stern. Uncle Takeo's image came up and said, "Take care of yourself," and he meant it. I thought of Grandma, as she always said, "Live strong." Then I was wondering and dreaming what would be the end of this journey but my decision was firm. "I will not disappoint you," I whispered, "so please wait for my return."

Nobuko age 14

From left: Uncle Takeo, his wife Nao,
Grandmother Chiyo - my father's mother,
cousins Shigeko and Miyoko

Fusako

The ship went out of Tokyo Bay and up through the queasy Bering Sea, the waves got bigger and I started to feel seasick. Just lying on a couch was meaningless but if I got up, I felt swaying and started to get nausea. So I closed my eyes and stayed lying down. "There is no alternative but to stick it out," I told myself.

Then I was remembering some of my past. Suddenly I said to myself "You know, I could have had a good-looking sister, but I don't. Why?"… the memories of why were gloomy. As Grandma often said "That poor little baby, she had such beautiful facial features. Her large eyes pronounced hope and her lips expressed words of something cheerful." Fusako lived for barely eight months and was gone.

Fusako was destined to leave us since the time she was only two weeks old. As repatriates (the people return to the country of origin due to the war end), we were directed to a freight train with no lights, no seats, no air, almost suffocating and we were crammed in all together. Mother ordered us, "Hold on to my hand tight. Never, never let go." We held each other's hands tight so as not to separate in the dark. I heard babies crying nearby and so was my baby sister. We got out of that train for transfer. We had about an hour or so to our last destination, Kure City, Hiroshima, which gave us a moment of relief. Mother brought the baby down from her papoose and laid her on her lap. Mother said aloud "Oh no, she is not breathing!" Grandma handed me an empty bottle, "Hurry, go get some water!" I ran to the water fountain and returned to Grandma. Immediately, Grandma sprayed the baby's face and wiped. She did this repeatedly. Gradually the baby gained consciousness and opened her eyes. Grandma grasping the baby's tiny fist said "It is a suffering time for all of us, but come with us poor little baby."

Later, on a July afternoon, when I was coming home from school, I saw a doctor leaving our house. Fusako had not been well. She was malnourished because my mother did not have enough milk to breast feed.

My brother Mitch and I sat by Fusako's bedside and held her hands. From her mouth, black liquid was leaking out and it trickled down to her soft baby cheeks then to her neck. Mitch and I took turns to wipe her. Mother could not bear to see Fusako in that condition, so she stood by the sink and washed dishes.

Grandma came home that day from work. She must have had an intuition of the tragedy so she was calm and gathered us around Fusako and we prayed together. The angel escorted her away to a better place.

I wondered if Fusako met our father in heaven. Both of them are there now. My father could have told Fusako how he was worried about the baby who was only a three month old fetus when he departed. Then I pictured my father saying, "My! I have a beautiful daughter now." "Daddy, the family now lives in Japan. Did you know that?"

"What, why?"

"The war is over and we had to go back home." They may be conversing, catching up on our events. They are alright now; I visualized our father comforting Fusako in his arms and they were contented. The only difference was that they were upstairs and we lived downstairs.

We understood, there is a reason for everything, so we accepted the way of God. Some memories are poignant however that is the way of life.

I must have been seasick a few days but once the body had become accustomed to its motion, I was alright and attended for the meals in the dining room.

A Month Long Journey

Although it was a freight ship, a few state-rooms were built in for the passengers. It was a nice room and the housekeeping was provided. I had the room all to myself with a shower and toilet, sofa and of course the bed. I enjoyed my porthole for peeking out, not that I saw anything out on the wide open water but only horizon. A slim closet in the corner of the room which was good enough to hang a few clothes since most of passengers would be there for matter of two weeks just to cross the Pacific Ocean. My case was not so, I was staying on until the ship docked in New York harbor.

There was a doctor who was invited to work along with American physicians in Minneapolis, a scientist who discovered something to do with cancer so he was given a fund to research further at a medical hospital in California, and a blind grandfather escorted by his grandson returning to live in Los Angeles.

There were a couple more people taking advantage of this sort of break. They were all nice people to keep company with and also they were the people who were going where they had to go within a budget. For the average people, airfares of those days were unthinkable. Imagine, in 1955 people were not flying around the world as today. At the first port, San Pedro, California, everybody carried their own bag, and saying goodbye, went off each on their own way. I was left alone behind but I knew my turn would come in another two weeks. Then it dawned on me, I was the only female on the ship. Not to be lonely, I chatted with a few friendly crewmembers. The captain seemed near retirement age. He was almost a father figure to me and kept his eye on me for the rest of my journey.

The ship went hugging the coast to the south. I stood by the stern, drawn to the breathtaking colorful scenery of California on the hill. The afternoon sun was shining on those red tile roofs while green lawns made contrast to create the perfect picture. "American image! I like it," I whispered and smiled. To my eyes, that was quite contrary to what I was used to in Japan. Right then I believed what I was seeing was the American personality: cheerful, friendly and pleasing in attitude. "Well, that's what I must merge into. Don't be so conservative. Relax! You are going to be Americanized." As I talked to myself, my fist pressed against the stern. "Okay, starting right now, change your personality!" Suddenly I was optimistic.

From the Pacific to Atlantic Ocean, going through the Panama Canal itself was an event but I was more captivated by that sunset. It was an amazing mix of red and orange – a huge fire ball phenomenon. The more I looked into that red, the more mysterious it became. But why? There was some charisma to it. Whatever it was, I felt I had to go beyond that horizon and capture it. "Yes, I am going to capture it. I am going for it. I am in a quest and I am striving because I am dedicated to conquer this challenge."

It was a month, a long journey, but it gave me time to think and contemplate my life.

New York

A mighty woman stood on a pedestal holding a torch in her right hand as the ship sailed into New York Harbor. With her silent lips she said, "Welcome" and opened the golden door for me. Wow, so this is New York! My eyes were peeled to the Manhattan skyline. I was full of excitement and purpose.

After a month on the sea I had finally made it to my destination. I always pictured that the woman stood right in the town square but instead she was standing on a small island. Is it the Statue of Liberty, really? I couldn't believe my own eyes. I warned myself, "See, things are not what you think. It's what you see, so you must be observant. Remember, now you are alone in another country."

As planned, Mr. Hoffman came to the ship to pick me up and he drove me to his home. He appeared to be in his late 30s and mostly bald.

"Honey!" Mr. Hoffman called out as we entered the door. A blonde woman looking to be in her mid 20s came walking down the hallway to meet us. Mr. Hoffman kissed her casually. It was known to me that this was the western manner of greeting but it was my first time witnessing anyone actually kissing.

"This is Nobuko. She finally got here," Mr. Hoffman introduced me to his wife.

"Did everything go alright?" she said looking at both of us. Her smile eased my tension.

Mr. Hoffman was fluent in Japanese but not Mrs. Hoffman, so I bowed. "How do you do," I said, with my prepared English sentence.

Mr. Hoffman patted my shoulder and introducing me to his wife said, "OKUSAN (wife) is a nice person, so you two should get along well, okay?" Then he said, "Honey, I have to get back to the office but where is the baby?"

"She is asleep in the backyard," Mrs. Hoffman pointed to the back of the house. I saw a baby carriage under a willow tree. Mr. Hoffman walked over and peeked into the carriage. He smiled with delight. In a hurried motion he kissed his wife again to say good-bye and left.

The moment Mr. Hoffman walked away, I felt helplessly detached from my family, own country, culture and language. Then quickly I realized the situation. A little voice from inside of me said, It doesn't matter anymore because you are already in another part of the world. Wasn't this the challenge you were well prepared for? "Yes, ma'am," I affirmed myself.

Mrs. Hoffman looked at the clock on the kitchen wall and said, "Well, it's lunch time." She took out the plates and opened a can of tuna fish. I took out a plate from another shelf. "Ooops," she said, "No, we have separate dishes for the diary and the meat. We have a kosher kitchen." I did not understand but I followed what she showed me.

We heard the baby cry. Mrs. Hoffman said, "Come, meet Samantha." She picked up the baby and said, "Hi, Samantha! Did you have a good nap? I love you!" She squeezed Samantha and handed her to me. I received Samantha in my arms like an important package. I remembered that Grandma had taught me how important it would be to value the baby and to be bonded. What she meant was that it would be good for my own future in the long run.

Since it was the first time I saw a Caucasian infant, somehow her face looked strange to me. Her pale skin and protruding nose brought to my mind the image of a white rabbit. Likewise, when she saw me, her eyes twitched and she jerked her tiny fists. Did I surprise her? Was she too young to have met any human from Asia? Nonetheless, I was her nanny. I carried her into the nursery changing her diaper. Oddly, the more I saw her, the more I was getting used to her features and her deep set eyes were no longer strange. I am going to devote my soul to her, I said to myself and hugged her tight. She chuckled.

In that afternoon the next-door neighbor dropped in to say hello. Mrs. Hoffman introduced me to her. "How do you pronounce your name again?" the neighbor asked. Honestly, I did not know how to answer soon enough in English. Mrs. Hoffman quickly cut in and said, "Nabico?" hesitantly and looked at me. I said "Nobuko!" They were mumbling between themselves and then decided to give me an American nickname. Penny, Joan, Anna, Kathy and a few more names were up. I said okay to "Kathy", not that it had any meaning to me. That's how swiftly I became a/k/a Kathy.

At dinner, this time it was Mrs. Hoffman's turn to introduce me to Mr. Hoffman, "Honey, this is Kathy."

My School Days

"I am going, going, going there, getting there," my heart raced with excitement. In my hand I carried a Japanese-English dictionary. It was so important for me to carry it everywhere I went because in 1955 the cellphone with translation app was not even dreamed of yet. It was my first day of school in America.

"Kathy Toyoda!" It was my name at the rollcall. "Yes, Sir," I answered with my stern posture and sincere respect to the teacher. However, some students were answering "Here" and waving their hand. The atmosphere seemed too friendly to me and it appeared that the students were not afraid of the teacher at all.

It was difficult for me to address the teacher as "you". The teacher was clearly my superior and therefore I wished to dignify his position by calling him by the title "teacher." Apparently, it was not culturally correct.

A year later, since my student visa was limited to only four years, I thought the secretarial course would be practical. So my typing skill was imperative. The timing worked out so that the typing room was vacant during my lunch period. The room was granted for me, all to myself. Every day, I went click, click, click on that Royal manual typewriter. Nowadays we call those typewriters antiques. My typing speed increased and I was happy.

One day, Dr. Cogger, the Principal, walking by the hallway caught sight of me from the window. "Hi, Kathy. What is going on that you are in the room all alone?" he drew the door open inquisitively.

"Hi, Dr. Cogger! This is my lunch period and I am practicing my typing."

"Oh, your lunch time! You should not be missing lunch."

"But I need the practice," I said.

Then the bell rang and I had to rush over to my next class. Dr. Cogger was impressed with my effort. He never forgot this incident, in fact he even mentioned it to the students at the assembly without referring to my name. His point was that each student should strive to make the most of their education toward success.

In my sophomore year, I enjoyed the Spanish class. Since it was a new language to the whole class, my lack of English did not matter. Even the syllables are very similar to Japanese so it came rather stress-free for me. So did the stenography class because it was just about catching sounds. Math was my least favorite class when I was in Japan. However thanks to that universal language, no matter where you are in the world, math is the same, so I did well in that class. I was comfortable in any subject in which the English language was not a significant part. In history class, a lot of reading was required so it was tough. American kids were exposed to more in European history and grew up with their own nation's history, whereas I was on the other side of the world. However, I did my utmost term by term, which put me on the honor roll a few times and I made the Hoffman family very proud.

At that time riding the school bus was like going on a sightseeing tour which gave me a good overlook of the area. The attitudes of American students on the bus were interesting. I watched everything for important aspects for me to learn. Some girls about 16, already dressed like women with makeup on their faces. Didn't they have some adolescent period in their life? I thought. Then there was a girl carrying a three-ring binder and I couldn't help noticing the cover. She had written in large letters, "I LOVE ELVIS", and it even had a kiss mark in red lipstick. She was showing it off, "Hey, look at my cover." "Oh, Elvis, I love him!" the girl next to me said. I was shocked how they openly and freely applied the word of LOVE. In Japanese society at least, the word of LOVE was used only in an intimate circumstance, and very seldom. Whenever they shouted, I listened very carefully and repeated the words silently to myself. It was a good opportunity to pick up American teen language and expressions, whether they were good or bad. I was just amazed at the way Americans express their personalities. On the other hand it helped me become a more open-hearted and open-minded person. Perhaps I was on the way to becoming Americanized.

With the support and kindness of my classmates, teachers, and everybody around, I made it through my school years. I never forgot that I was a guest in America and must behave with gratitude and represent the best of my country.

Graduation

Discovering Jewish Holidays

"What a spectacular scene!" I was startled. The neighborhood was lit up lavishly in the evening of December.

"When are we going to decorate the house for Christmas?" I asked Mrs. Hoffman. "No, we don't celebrate Christmas. We are Jewish," said Mrs. Hoffman. Her poise showed self-respect. That's when I learned of the existence of multiple religions in the U.S.A.

Instead of a Christmas tree in the house, we had a menorah with eight candles. In the spring came Passover and I was introduced to matzah. The sheet of cracker tasted plain. It went good with a spread of butter and a little sprinkle of salt. I took a plate of macaroons to visit Jewish friends, since I knew they were a Passover treat. Everyone laughed. I took them by surprise. They thought, "What does a Japanese girl know about macaroons for Passover," but I knew.

Even today, I get hungry for those Jewish foods: matzah, gefilte fish, pickled herring, borscht, and latkes to name a few.

Soon after the school started in the fall, it was Rosh Hashanah, the Jewish New Year. All the Jewish students were observing the holidays. Since the Hoffman family gathered at Mrs. Hoffman's parents' home in Brooklyn, I was happy to join. Anyway they were delighted to have me help with baby Samantha and in the kitchen. "Happy New Year!" I greeted the family. When I returned to the school with an absentee note, teachers asked if I was a Jewish. I just shrugged my shoulders.

Yom Kippur followed a few days after Rosh Hashanah. That holiest day, they fast and let go of sins. The people around looked more serious on that day. Samantha and I were excused from the strict fasting but I tried to be discreet. Since I was here in America, I wanted to experience whatever there was.

I never expected to be so involved in Jewish holidays before, however living with my sponsor's family four years gave me good insights. I remember the first day of my arrival, how I was puzzled about the kosher kitchen but now I understood.

Years later at one of my office Christmas parties, I sang Dayeinu, Dayeinu (a Jewish holiday song) which made my Jewish comrades burst out laughing. Someone pointed to a small Christmas tree and said, "Is that a Chanukah bush?" I said, "If you believe so." After all, many religions exist in the U.S.A. but I think religion is whatever you believe in honestly.

Oh, Grandma

Grandma said, "Live strong!" Those were the last words I remember from her when I left Japan in 1955.

A year later, 1956, my first year of high school was over. That day, I waited for the mail as usual. Receiving a letter from home was my sole comfort. However that day's mail brought me a devastating message.

My cousin wrote, "So sorry about your grandmother. We knew you and your grandmother were very close, but keep your courage up. We look forward to your coming home in three years."

What? I was startled. Was he saying my Grandma died? I had a hard time accepting the fact but more condolences arrived to confirm the truth.

Now I have nothing but the stories she used to tell me. I remember what Grandma often said about how the Japanese Imperial Power was feared by all the regions in Asia until it was defeated in WWII in 1945. Korea was one of Japan's colonies and many citizens of Japan had ventured out there to settle. My Grandma and Grandfather were among them, looking for a challenge. In 1923, as they were crossing the water of Tsushima Strait to Busan, Korea, they held a precious little toddler who would be my mother, Teruko.

They established themselves a comfortable living but while enjoying their new region, he became ill and left my Grandma as a widow. At his bedside, she wept and pledged to the beloved husband that she would carry on his burden of protecting their daughter, and she said goodbye to him. Despite being brokenhearted, Grandma grew resilient in bringing up my mother to be a fine Japanese lady.

As was the culture and the tradition, an arranged marriage was offered for my mother and father. My mother, like most Japanese young ladies had a tutor for floral arrangement and tea ceremony. That tutor's husband was my father's superior in the government office and they became my parents' matchmakers. Grandma was so proud of her goal of providing a fine wedding for my mother. Grandma thought from then on she could relax and look forward to the grandchildren in the near future. However life does not go the way you have planned.

I can recall things started to go bad as they say, when it rains it pours. My father passed away. To make matters worse, Mom was in her first trimester of pregnancy. Then the news radio aired, "The war has ended and we are defeated." Some people cried because they felt betrayed by their government. I remember the radio stayed on for a few more days and then communication for us was cut off, leaving us in the dark and to unknown future. We were in the midst of confusion and helpless with no law and order. We simply walked away from everything to go home to Japan. We arrived our destination, where Grandma grew up and familiar. When Grandma heard American occupation forces were coming to build their barracks, she hurried to apply and got a job as a housekeeper. As for Mom, too much of unfortunate occurrences led her to adjustment disorder and difficult for her to hold on to a job thus we lived on Grandma's steady income.

When I observed Grandma working so hard, I felt compelled to do something to show her my gratitude. Grandma was a smoker but that was an unaffordable luxury to her at the time. Realizing she could no longer enjoy her habit, I sympathized for her. I went on the street to pick up cigarette butts. I waited for Grandma to come home from work and proudly showed her the pile of cigarette butts in the palms of my hands. She smiled and said, Arigato (thank you) that was the reward for me. However, I knew that inside Grandma's heart was weeping, saying, "Why is this happening?"

Grandma meant everything to me.

Losing Grandma was devastating, but the bonding we had was vital. It was she, Hanayo Toyoda who gave me strength and helped to shape my life. Her words "Live strong!" are always leading me through my life.

Grandma, mom, and Grandpa

Mom's Fate

The fall of 1959, I couldn't be more excited about going home to Japan.

A flash of memory went by. "Don't hurt … Mom, I am here!" That is one incident I try to disconnect from my recollections, yet it lingered still.

"Help! Mom will kill us!" I can still see that eight inch chef's knife coming at my face. I was seven years old and my brother Mitch was five. Grabbing Mitch's hand, I rushed out of the house. "Mom will kill us!" hardly breathing I screamed louder, looking for someone who would hear me and come to the rescue. A few neighbors came out to see what it was all about. Mitch and I rushed into Mrs. Suzuki's arms. "Tasukete!" I cried out in Japanese, "Help!" I held Mitch to my body tightly and protectively. My heart was pounding. "What happened?" asked Mrs. Suzuki, turning her head to observe the surroundings.

"It's okay, it's okay. Come on home," my mother came calling after us, her eyes gleaming fiercely. Mom was obviously most uncomfortable and embarrassed in front of her neighbors. An eerie feeling fell in the atmosphere for a moment, as Mitch and I still hid in fear behind Mrs. Suzuki.

Mom seemed returning to her senses. Her expression had changed, as if saying, "Why should they walk back with me now?" What happened was unacceptable but Mom could not understand what came over her.

In a few moments everyone calmed down, then we went home. She glanced at that chef's knife… "Did I try to stab my children with this knife? Why?" Casually, she put it back in the kitchen drawer and then held her head, sinking down to the floor. It was the postnatal psychosis; it came and went like bipolar disorder depression.

I took pity on her for her situation: First she was brought up knowing nothing but living in the gentle world as if she was a princess. However the time came when all the unfortunate events crushed into us. My father deceased and while we were still grieving, WWII ended in Japanese defeat. The post-war chaos drew us into a dark and uncertain future. Then followed my baby sister's death. Those occurrences, one after another, were too many tough challenges to overcome for Mom who never expected the world to be so misgiving. Thus her mind shattered and never mended totally.

My brother and I were learning to cope, carefully living with such a hurtful and complicated relationship with mother. Incidents were forgiven. After all, Mom was still our mother and things happened because of her brain disease. I prayed to God every night that Mom's illness would just vanish away like spells or magic. That was not likely, so we had to embrace and deal with the situation. So it would just be an intriguing mystery and test of life which makes us that much stronger. Don't they say, "After the storm comes the sunshine"? Our conviction was to endure the storm and wait until we see the sunshine, believing life goes on with determination and trust.

Even when I had an opportunity to attend four years of high school in the U.S.A. and could have enjoyed more years, my mother's circumstance always hindered me going for more. My mind was to do something about our situation or at least be with the family to witness and possibly be a comfort.

As my high school graduation approached, my heart was racing with the thought of returning home.

My parents' wedding

Home Sweet Home

With the sound of a whistle the train was pulling out from Kure Station near Hiroshima. My eyes flooded with tears, then I choked up. It was one of my life's most poignant moments.

Five years later that feeling was hitting my heart again. My high school graduation was over three months ago, thus I was due to go home. I wanted desperately to reunite with my family. I remember the days when Grandma was the breadwinner for us. Since her passing, my constant worry was how my brother Mitch and Mom were making their living.

The Hoffmans were telling me to be patient until they got someone after me. I appreciated the Hoffmans liking me and needing me, however, I had to get on with my own life. It was my trust and hope that I would be going home as soon as I finished my four years of high school, but it did not seem to be that way. With my anxiety and worry I was frustrated, and I busted out crying. As a result, the Hoffmans realized my rights and that I had to return home. My flight reservation was made quickly to fly out in a few days. Yes, this time I was going by air instead of by sea. Flying had become the new standard of travel since the time I came to America in 1955. The thought of finally going home the next day was indescribable.

In the morning, I dressed my little Samantha in a blue and green checked cotton dress which I ironed the previous night for her. "This is the last time I am ironing for Samantha," I said to myself and I felt a bit blue. Mrs. Hoffman called Samantha over and told her the news that I was leaving to go home. Samantha stood dumbfounded with a sad expression. She gave me a hug which felt like it went on for an hour. She was already going on six years old.

With so much anticipation, over 13 hours of flight was not too long for me. "Welcome to Tokyo," the flight attendant's voice was heard. At last I was home! This time not counting Grandma in the family was odd. After Grandma passed away, Mom went to live with my father's sister in Nagoya and my brother was in Tokyo with Uncle Takeo's family. We were living in all different directions losing the structure of a family composition. For that, I felt guilty because of my absence and I wanted so badly to make up for those missed few years.

The very next day of returning home to Japan, I visited Mr. Naka's office for his advice on where I should find a job immediately. Mr. Naka's concern for me was more than I can ever repay. It was he who sparked my dream of coming to the U.S.A. in 1954.

After I found a job, I hopped on a train the first long weekend, to go retrieve my mom. Finally we were a family again. My brother was already working and Mom stayed home to do the house chores. I happily went to work for the pharmaceutical company Japan Upjohn. It was newly formed as a joint venture with Sumitomo, one of Japan's well-known businesses. Those were the most fulfilling, treasured, and gratifying days of my life.

While I was indulging myself in the joy of reunified family life, something dawned on me. "What is my future?" Before I realized it, I was 21 years old. As much as I respected my homeland, culture and memories, I started to feel there was a cavity in my mind. I missed American freedom. That is, I could be whoever and whatever I wanted to be there, whereas Japanese culture looks at people based on social status. There were many behavioral restrictions in order for me to fit in. I chewed over the subject then I foresaw that it would take me some time to melt back into Japanese society. Isn't that the irony that human nature seems to be never satisfied, always looking for more? I was home only ten months but I saw Mom and my brother were getting along alright. I felt the time had come to take care of myself. My heart started to yearn for returning to New York. I left my family again but kept the family bond with me.

My American Dream

People say you can be anything you want to be in this country – the American Dream. So this was a test to see if I could do it, too.

On October 16, 1961, I was like a free bird out of the cage. Deep in my heart however, there was a gloomy spot that was the guilt of deserting the Hoffmans. I never deny that the Hoffmans were my American family. Nevertheless I kept telling myself, I did what I had to do at the time, so put that thought away for now. I went on the subway to go to work.

My first day of work at the Marubeni Company, I grasped my power, I trusted my capability and quickly made some good friends in the office. Olivia Deliniekos, who sat next to me, gave me friendly hints about how to get around the office. Eventually we became close friends. It was a big Japanese company and I felt big too.

My pay was $72.00 a week and from that I managed to pay $15.00 each week for a rooming house, bought my own groceries, and sent $50.00 each month to my Mom. That Christmas I rewarded myself with a RCA portable television. My only furniture was an old four-drawer chest about 30 inches wide, 30 inches high and 15 inches deep. I placed the television on it and made it my own theater. The screen was only black and white then. I was so proud of myself for that accomplishment.

As a busy bee and a penny-pincher, I needed more than my full-time job to feel fulfilled and content. Looking for a part-time job, I almost had a weekend position at Rockefeller Center in Manhattan as a tour guide. However, I was reminded by my employer that the Immigration Law prohibited me having a second job, since the Marubeni Company was legally my sole supporter. The personnel director said that if I was not satisfied with my pay, they could just let me go. Oh, no! I needed to keep Marubeni as my sponsor to stay in this country. I was appreciative for the position given to me by my employer and I had no right to have another job. But one day I stumbled upon an executive family newly arrived from Japan. I was asked if I would tutor their children with their homework. I gladly accepted and the children did very well. Their gratuities provided me with extra income. Our friendship lasted for many years after.

I had moved five times in one year, starting with a rooming house then living with roommates and searching for a decent apartment. Tired of moving and wanting to settle down, I was 23 years old. Then there was Bill, a true confidante since we had met at Times Square two years earlier. However we were not engaged nor did we have any concrete plan ahead together. I felt comfortable with him and felt I could always lean on him for the help when I needed to.

I had a conversation with myself about the direction of my life, and Grandma's image came up. She said, "Watch out for the guys who drink and gamble." I appreciated her advice. Bill did not drink nor gamble. She asked if he had a good steady job. I answered, "Yes, indeed. Would you approve of him?" I inquired. To that she nodded and smiled then faded away.

I knew the ultimate decision was up to me, yet I missed the presence of my family. No matter what I had done, I was responsible for my own life and that had been my way since I was 15.

Thanks to the American Dream, I was already independent. No matter how small my dream was, I was free and happy. My own way of pursuing life was the American Dream for me.

Our courtship

August 5, 1963

There was a transparent plastic box in the refrigerator. Inside were a large white orchid and roses with the spray of baby's breath. "This is the day! This is the most spirited corsage of my life." The overwhelming tears filled my eyes and heart.

The white summer dress I was putting on was not an iconic Vera Wang nor from David's Bridal Shop. It was a simple cotton dress which I purchased a couple of months ago in Macy's Manhattan. It was a practical and economic decision because I can wear it even after I get married. I carefully put on a white pillbox hat with netting covering my forehead. Now! I said looking into the mirror, Is this okay? I heard my grandmother's voice say, "You look lovely. Go on and celebrate your wedding day." Thank you, I murmured. I must admit that I was feeling a bit low. I was lonely, realizing that I had no one to escort me out from my apartment. It's your big day;

remember, you are going to get married. My eyes moistened with emotion. Be strong – don't let your tears mess up your mascara. Now come on, I lectured myself and locked the door.

The fact was that many girls from foreign countries were in the same situation in those days, in the early '60s – their weddings were like mine. Most of us could not afford to have the family fly in from their mother country and be together to celebrate a fancy reception.

I took the subway to Jamaica Station where the courthouse was located. Olivia Deliniekos, my friend from my work, and Thomas Clements, who was Bill's buddy from military service in Korea, stood for us as the witnesses. We were married in the Office of Civil Marriage. The Performance of Marriage Ceremony certificate was three dollars.

The corsage was pinned to my white dress. A boutonniere was pinned on Bill's dark jacket lapel. "Take pictures!" Click, click. We were a nice smiling couple. I felt pretty on that momentous day and Bill looked handsome, too.

It is remarkable that Bill and I have been married over a half a century. I recall how I wanted my marriage to be a success, especially when this was all up to me. My family was far away on the other side of the globe. Of course the main factors were the racial and cultural differences. I asked myself, "How independent should I be?" My determination was to be able to face my family without any embarrassments, mistakes, and regrets whatsoever. My obligation was to exhibit the best of my best attitudes, as the best possible wife. It would be a flower blossoming on my new family tree. "You see, the Japanese makes the best wife. She is the best we acquired in our family," I wanted my in-laws to say. I wanted to hear the sound of "Good job" from my family back in Japan. My intuition kept on telling me to go humble. My desire would become reality.

All I wanted was to be legally joined and to have a better marriage than a wedding.

After 50 some years of marriage, here I am in Florida and grateful. Lying on a chaise lounge by the pool, I am looking at a cloud and its shape. I call out, "There! Bill and I." Whether it is just my imagination or not, I keep on believing. Was it our destiny when we met in Times Square in the spring of 1961 under the illusion of giant smoke rings by the Camel Cigarette billboard? The American

dream was necessary to have it come true –
"My marriage."

Our wedding day

www.ingramcontent.com/pod-product-compliance
Lightning Source LLC
LaVergne TN
LVHW091209080426
835509LV00006B/907